Beethoven Ludwig Van

Piano Sonatas

21°"Waldstein" - 22° 23°"Appassionata" - 24° - 25° - 26°

ISBN-SKU: 9781802210286

Content

Piano Sonata No.21 in C major, op.53 "Waldstein" — page 3

Piano Sonata No.22 in F major, op.54 — page 35

Piano Sonata No.23 in F minor, op.57 "Appassionata" — page 50

Piano Sonata No.24 in F# major, op.78 — page 79

Piano Sonata No.25 in G major, op.79 — page 89

Piano Sonata No.26 in E flat major, op.81° — page 98

SONATE.
Op. 53.
Dem Grafen von Waldstein gewidmet.

1) The fingering in italics and the pedal indications are Beethoven's.

1) The original edition shows: [musical example] Both the b^3 and the d^3 are engraving errors; if Beethoven had intended the d^3, he would have had to make it the first note of the measure (2nd 16th).

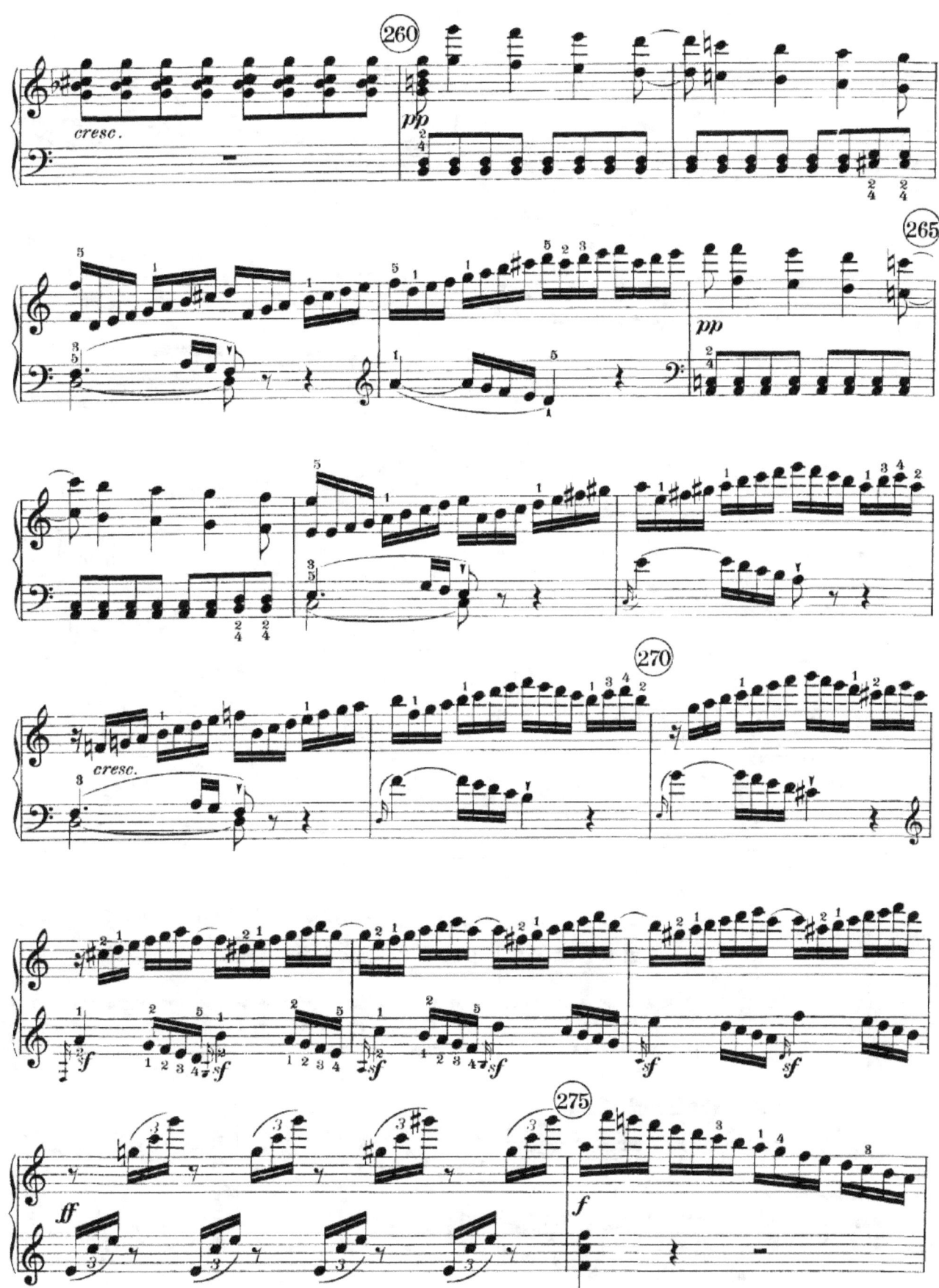

1) May be played as approximately 6 quarter-beats

INTRODUZIONE.
Adagio molto.

RONDO.
Allegretto moderato.

Attacca subito il Rondo:

1) The intention of Beethoven's long pedals, which take no account of dissonant passing chords or mixtures, is a spiritual, almost transcendental, binding-together of larger groups, which his instrument also favored (cf. Op. 31, No. 2, first movement, mm. 143–148 & 153–158). On modern instruments one may try to achieve this effect by half-pedaling at the passing harmonies (mm. 3, 7, 11, 15, etc.), a kind of legatissimo of the pedal, comparable to legato playing in general.
2) The pp at G_1 serves to identify the opening of the motif. 3) Thus in the original edition; some later ones give g^2 in place of f^2.

1) The first 16th note is detached to identify the opening of the motif. 2) Trill starting with the upper note in 32nds. 3) As Beethoven indicates at mm. 490 ff., the trill starting with the upper note is to be played uninterruptedly in 32nds. The fingering given makes this easy to execute.

1) The two 8th-rests in place of a quarter-rest, and the ※ directly below the fourth 8th-beat, are based on the original edition

1) Usual simplification.

SONATA

Op. 54.

Composta nel 1805, pubblicata in aprile 1806 presso il "Bureau des arts et de l'industrie„ di Lipsia.

(a) L'edizione originale aveva questo "gruppetto-mordente", che si incontra pure in altri lavori di B.: nell'Op. 78, nella Sonata per Violoncello Op. 5, N.º 2 e nella Sonata per Violino Op. 12, N.º 1. Esso si dovrà eseguire così: ecc., oppure (più agevole):

(a) L'édition originale avait ici ce "gruppetto-mordant", qu'on rencontre aussi dans d'autres oeuvres de B.: dans l'Op. 78, dans la Sonate pour Violoncelle Op. 5, N.º 2, et dans la Sonate pour Violon Op. 12, N.º 1. On doit l'exécuter ainsi: ou bien (plus facile):

(a) The original edition had here this "turn-mordent" which is also to be met with in other works of Beethoven:— in Op. 28, in the Sonata for Violoncello, in the Sonata for Violin, Op. 12, N.º 1. It should be played thus: or (easier) thus:

(a) Quasi tutte le edizioni antiche e moderne hanno questa versione erronea:
Presque toutes les éditions anciennes et modernes ont cette version erronée:
Nearly all the ancient and modern editions have this erroneous version:

(a) Questo *p* improvviso, cancellato nelle edizioni móderne, figurava sulle originali. Non vedo ragione alcuna per sopprimerlo, ma credo che si debba completarlo con un brevissimo ⟨⟩ per condurre al *ff*

(b) Durata della 𝄐 : 5 ♩;

(c) Idem: 6 ♩ (in tempo non rallentato).

(a) Ce *p* subit, effacé dans les éditions modernes, figurait sur les originales. Je ne vois aucune raison pour le supprimer, mais je crois qu'il doit être complété par un léger ⟨⟩ pour conduire au *ff*

(b) Durée du 𝄐 : 5 ♩;

(c) idem: 6 ♩ (sans ralentir).

(a) This sudden *p*, omitted in the modern editions, figured in the original editions. I see no reason for omitting it, but think it should be completed by a slight ⟨⟩ in order to lead up to *ff*.

(b) Duration of 𝄐 : 5 ♩;

(c) idem: 6 ♩ (in time, without "rallentando").

(a) Per agevolare il legato in questa difficilissima battuta, uso ed insegno da tempo la seguente versione:

Pour faciliter le legato dans cette mesure si difficile, j'emploie et j'enseigne la version suivante:

In order to facilitate the *legato* in this most difficult bar, I employ and teach the following version:

(a) Il trillo senza finale, cioè come lo scrisse l'autore.

(a) Le trille sans terminaison, c'est à dire comme l'écrivit l'auteur.

(a) The trill without an ending, as the composer wrote it.

(a) Altra diteggiatura: Questa ha la mia preferenza, ma è consigliabile soltanto agli esecutori avanzati.

(a) Autre doigté: Celui-ci a ma préférence, mais il n'est conseillable qu'aux exécutants avancés.

(a) Another fingering: This has my preference, but is recommended only to advanced players.

(a) Anche questo trillo dev'essere eseguito senza finale.

(a) Ce trille aussi doit être exécuté sans terminaison.

(a) This trill also should be played without an ending.

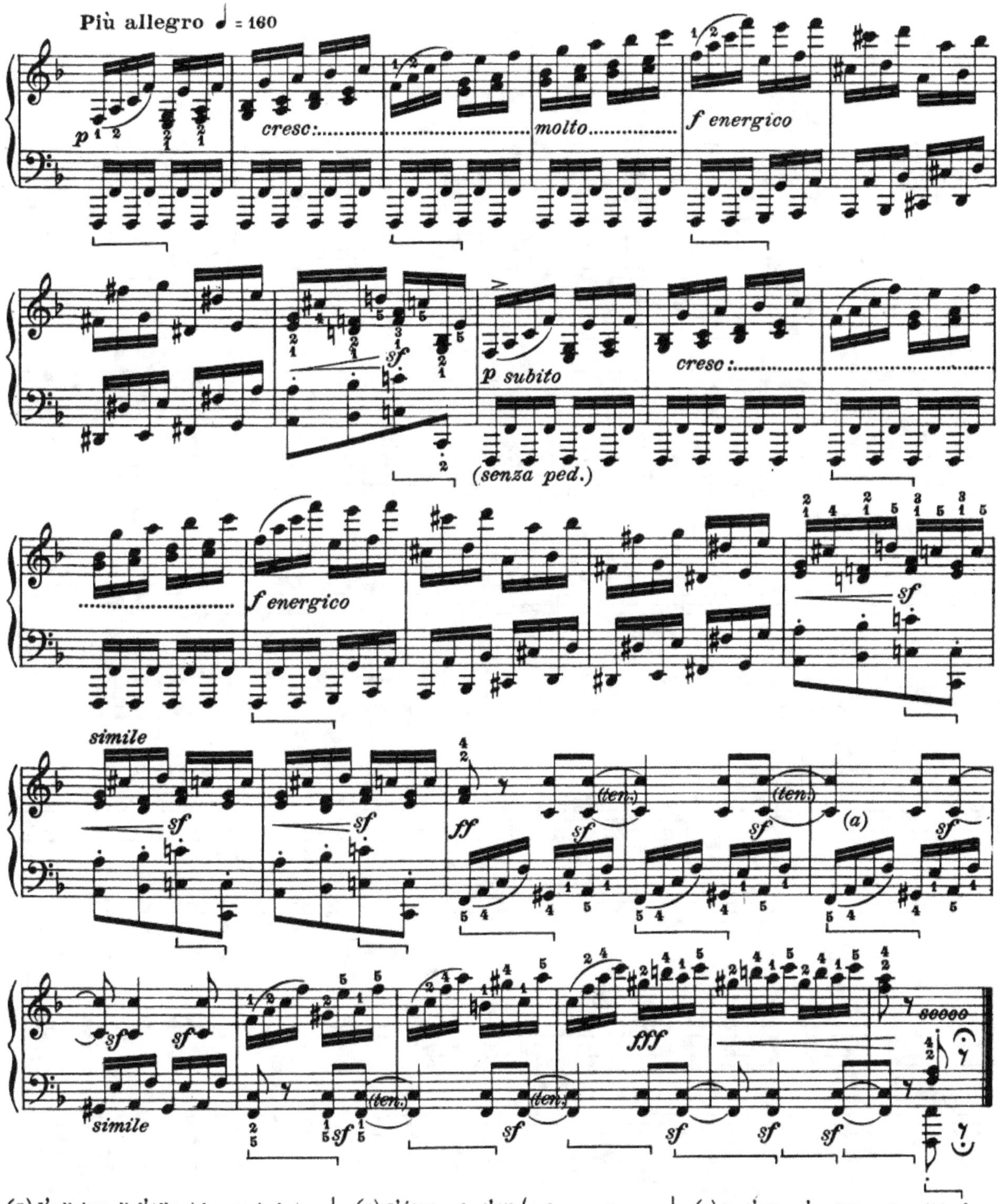
Più allegro ♩ = 160
p
cresc:
molto
f energico
sf
p subito
(senza ped.)
cresc:
f energico
sf
simile
sf
ff
(ten.)
(a)
simile
fff

(*a*) L'edizione di d'Albert ha questa battuta e la seguente, nella m.d., conformi all'edizione originale, la quale era testualmente:

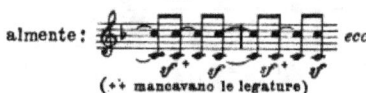

ecc.
(++ mancavano le legature)

Però le battute seguenti, colle parti invertite, dimostrano esaurientemente l'errore primitivo. Perciò non ho creduto di adottare la versione di d'Albert.

(*a*) *L'édition de d'Albert donne cette mesure et la suivante conformes à l'original pour la m.d.: textuellement ceci:*

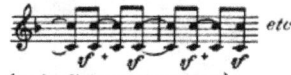

etc.
(++ les liaisons manquaient)

Pourtant les mesures suivantes, avec les parties interverties, démontrent absolument l'erreur primitive. Aussi n'ai-je pas cru devoir adopter la version de d'Albert.

(*a*) E. d'Albert's edition gives this bar and the following to the right hand, in accordance with the original edition, which was textually thus:

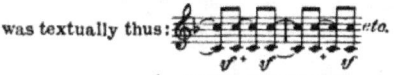

etc.
(++ the ties were missing)

However, the following bars, with the parts inverted, demonstrate the initial error. For this reason I have decided not to adopt d'Albert's version

SONATE.
Op. 57.
Dem Grafen Franz von Brunswick gewidmet.

Allegro assai.

23.

1) The pedal indications are Beethoven's. 2) Trill from below, with an anticipation (c²) inserted into the Nachschlag: The shortest execution perhaps thus. 3) In the autograph and original edition (Bureau des Arts, Vienna) the trill has no addition to it; here one might add g² as a short appoggiatura. 4) Only the original grouping of the arpeggio fits the musical meaning.

1) In the autograph and original edition, e³ instead of f♭².

1) In this measure and in m. 160 only the written-out simple Nachschlag is permitted, not the form in m. 156 or 162.

1) In the autograph and original edition, no addition to the trill. 2) Cf. the footnote to m. 45.

1) In mm. 204-205 & 206-207 the 16th-note figure on the first and second quarter-beats—over the long halfnotes in the l. h.—represents 3 x 4 sixteenths; with the beginning of the motif in the l. h., each group of six sixteenths forms a unit. Therefore, to reproduce on the last two quarter-beats the figuration of the first two, as printed in many editions, contradicts the musical meaning.

1) This exact reproduction of the autograph and original edition from m. 227 to m. 234 excludes a distribution of the music between both hands. The fingering supplied within parentheses is a suggested simplification through use of the l. h.

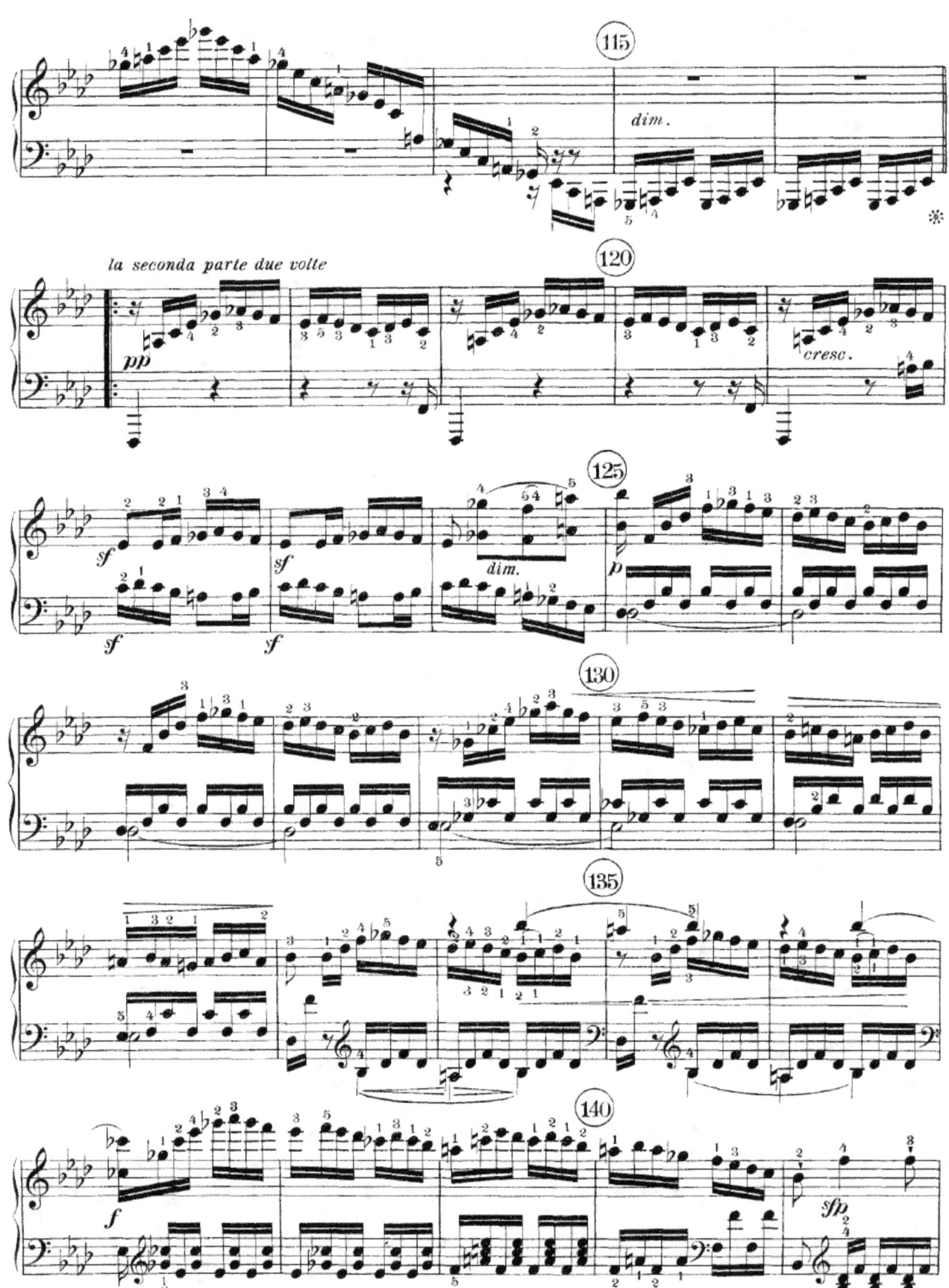

1) The tie clearly in the autograph.

1) In the autograph there is a natural sign before the D in mm. 291 & 295.

Sonate.
Op. 78.

Der Gräfin Therese von Brunswick gewidmet.

Componiert im Oktober 1809.

1) The fingering in italics and the pedal indications are Beethoven's.
2) Here, in contrast to Op. 54 (cf. 1st movement, mm. 18, 20 & 24), a true *prallender Doppelschlag* is wanted:
3) In the autograph and original edition (Breitkopf & Härtel) the l. h. has *g* instead of *f* ✕ in this measure and the next.

1) See footnote to m. 17. 2) In the autograph and original edition the l. h. has *c* instead of *b♯*.

1) It is unacceptable here to repeat the f♯ of the second quarter-beat, since the third g¹–e¹ has motivic significance; see the thirds e²–c♯², d²–b¹ and b¹–g♯¹ in the following measures.

1) The l.h. over the r.h.

1) This measure, in a way, amounts to four 8ths: C♯, c♯, c♯¹ and the 8th-rest.

Sonate.
Op. 79.

1) The pedal indications are Beethoven's. 2) Thus in the original edition (Breitkopf & Härtel); the difference between the harmonic anticipations in this measure and in mm. 56 & 127 is intentional.

1) See footnote to m. 5.
2) Here still *forte*, in contrast to the *piano* group in mm. 66–74; mm. 83–89 stand in the same *forte–piano* contrast to mm. 90–98.

1) See footnote to m. 5. 2) The 3 notes of the turn fall in the 2nd quarter-beat.

1) Long appoggiatura, thus equal to a 16th.

Sonate.
Op. 81ª
Das Lebewohl.

Bei der Abreise S. K. Hoheit des verehrten Erzherzogs Rudolph. Wien, am 21. Mai 1809.*

*) "On the departure of H. M. the revered Archduke Rudolph. Vienna, May 21, 1809." (The French entered Vienna in 1809.) In opposition to Beethoven's specific instructions, the original edition bears a title he complained of several times: "Sonate caractéristique: Les adieux, l'absence, et le retour" (The Farewell, The Absence, The Return—Das Lebewohl, Abwesenheit, Wiedersehen).

1) The fingering in italics and the pedal indications are Beethoven's.

1) In the autograph there is a *p* here too, in place of the erased ⇒

6 1) The slur here follows the autograph and the original edition in its difference from mm 23 & 24

1) Here the slur is once more like mm 23 & 24, again on the basis of the autograph and original edition.

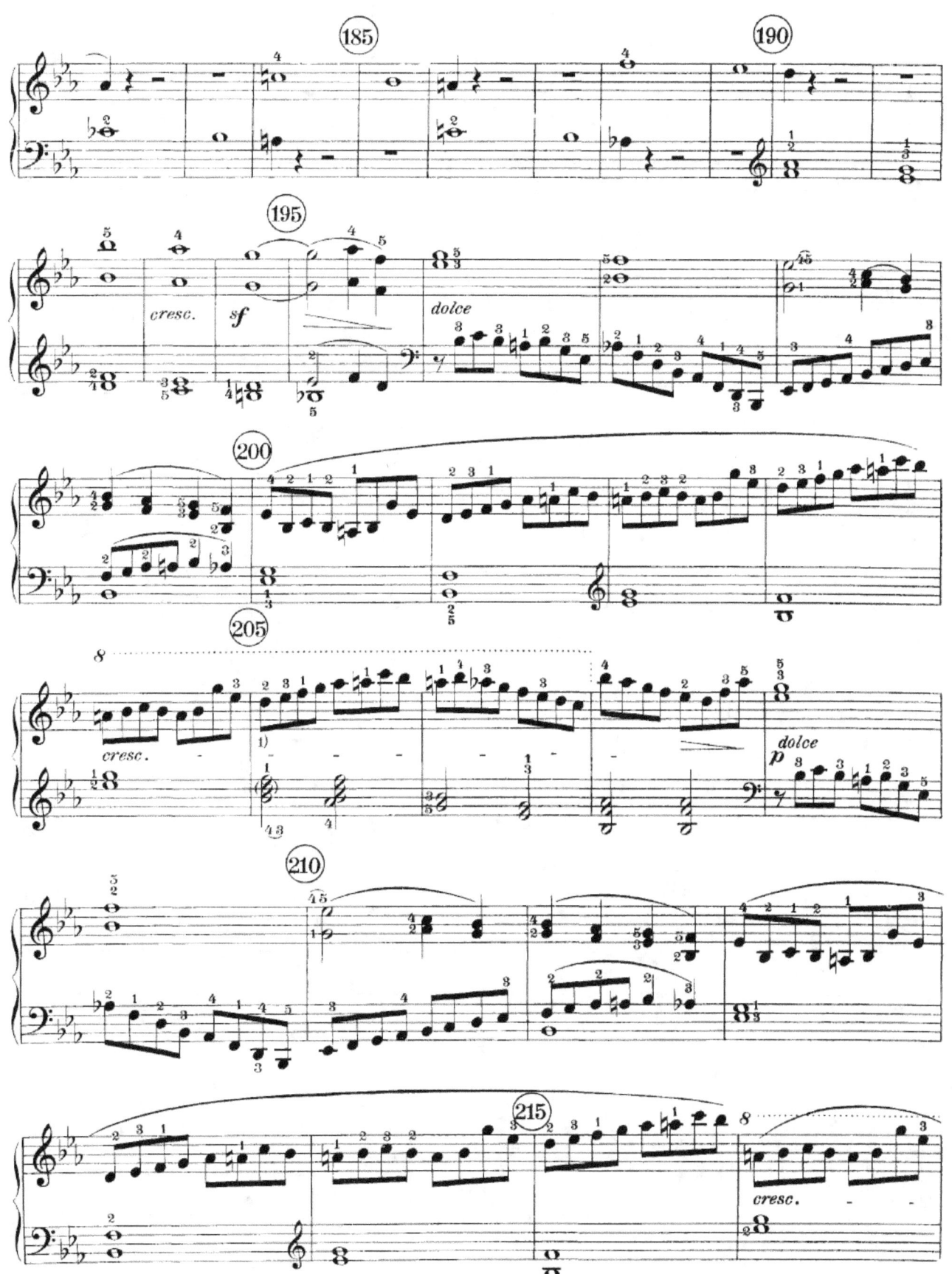

1) d^2 in the l. h. chord according to the autograph.

Abwesenheit.
Andante espressivo.
In gehender Bewegung, doch mit Ausdruck.

1) Execute the ornament (*prallender Doppelschlag*) before the second 8th-beat
2) Execute the ornament on the fourth 32nd-beat.
3) Beethoven was obviously thinking of a *prallender Doppelschlag* ornamented in trill-like fashion

Wiedersehen.
Vivacissimamente.
Im lebhaftesten Zeitmaasse.

Im Januar 1810.

1) Trill with the Nachschlag bb^1 c^2.

SONATE.

Op. 90.

Dem Grafen Moritz von Lichnowsky gewidmet.

Componiert im August 1814.

Mit Lebhaftigkeit und durchaus mit Empfindung und Ausdruck.*

*) Lively, with feeling and expression throughout.
1) The l h below the r. h.

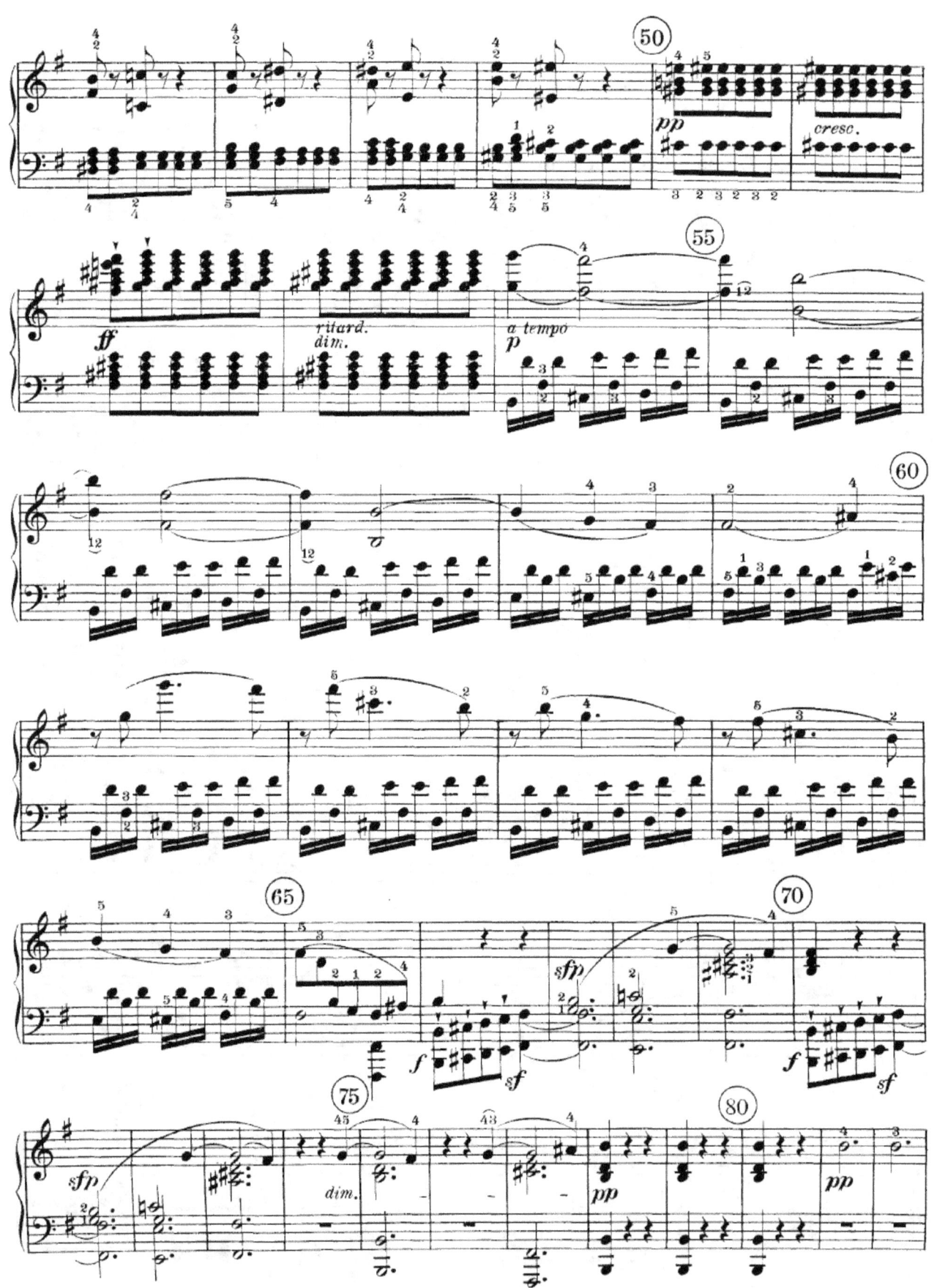

1) The l. h. below the r. h.

1) In the original edition (Steiner, Vienna) this chord lacks the *a¹*.
2) In the original edition the first 8th note has no octave.

Nicht zu geschwind und sehr singbar vorzutragen.*

*) To be played not too fast and very songfully.
1) The repetition of this group of measures, in mm. 17–24, is characterized not only by the octave reinforcement but also by the variant of the neighboring note g♯ in m 21.

1) See footnote to m. 13.

1) In the original edition the e^1 is a quarter note, not an 8th. 2) In the original edition the $f\sharp^1$ is a quarter note, not an 8th.

1) See footnote to m. 13.

1) In the original edition the *B* in the bass is a quarter note. 2) In the original edition this chord has $f\#°$, not $d\#°$ as in recent editions.

1) & 2) In the original edition the 2 b's are not tied between measures.
3) The failure to recognize the 2nd imitation (g#¹–f#¹–c²–c²) between mm. 284 & 285 is the cause of the incorrect slurs in all editions. In the original edition the execution of the correct slur is faulty.

www.ingramcontent.com/pod-product-compliance
Lightning Source LLC
Chambersburg PA
CBHW081620100526
44590CB00021B/3522